MAGGIE SMITH: A LEGENDARY EXIT

The Final Curtain Call of Cinema's
Unmatched Grande Dame, and the Legacy
She Left Behind

Shirley R. Benz

COPYRIGHT ©

All rights reserved. No part of this publication may be reproduced, distributed, or transmitted in any form or by any means, including photocopying, recording, or other electronic or mechanical methods, without the prior written permission of the publisher, except in the of brief questions embodied in the critical reviews and use certain other noncommercial user permitted by copyright law.

Copyright © **Shirley R. Benz**, *2024.*

Preface

In the realm of theater and movies, few names generate a feeling of awe and veneration quite like **Dame Maggie Smith.** Across an extraordinary career that lasted over seven decades, she graced theaters and screens with performances that ***grabbed hearts, moved minds,*** and left indelible fingerprints on the world of acting. From her magnificent depiction of ***Jean Brodie*** to her humorous personification of ***the Dowager Countess in Downton Abbey*** and ***the wise Professor McGonagall in Harry Potter,*** Maggie Smith's personas were bigger than life frequently as legendary as the lady herself.

The objective of this book is to highlight the life of Dame Maggie Smith beyond the roles she played. This is not simply a celebration of her art but an insight inside the lady who, with elegance, humor, and an unending devotion to the trade, quietly revolutionized acting. Her incredible journey, her great ***humility***, and her ***unwavering professionalism*** even in the face of obstacles are all part of the wider tale that this book aims to unearth.

As we examine the stages of her career and life, including her last bow, we recognize her great contribution to the arts. Maggie Smith's impact transcends the honors and critical praise her work lives on in the performances that continue to inspire, challenge, and move audiences worldwide.

This biography is an homage to Dame Maggie Smith, the lady behind the art, and an invitation for readers to go with her, one last time, through the life of a legend.

MAGGIE SMITH: A LEGENDARY EXIT

The Final Curtain Call of Cinema's Unmatched Grande Dame, and the Legacy She Left Behind

Shirley R. Benz

ABOUT THE AUTHOR

 I am Shirley R. Benz, a passionate storyteller and accomplished author, devoted to crafting engaging narratives and insightful articles. With a keen eye for detail and a deep understanding of human emotions, I write across a variety of genres, capturing the complexities of life in my unique and compelling voice.

My interest in writing began at a young age, fueled by my love for literature and my desire to explore the world through words.

Over the years, I have honed my craft, developing a distinctive style that resonates with both readers and critics. My stories often delve into themes of identity, relationships, and the intricate dance of everyday life, offering a window into the nuanced experiences of my characters.

In addition to fiction, I am also an accomplished essayist and journalist, contributing thought-provoking articles to various publications. My work in nonfiction reflects my curiosity about the world and my commitment to shedding light on important issues with clarity and compassion.

I am happily married and find great joy and inspiration in my personal life. Balancing my writing career with the support and encouragement of my spouse, who shares my love for storytelling and creativity, is a true blessing. Together, we enjoy exploring new places, discovering hidden stories, and savoring the simple moments that make life extraordinary.

As I continue my journey as a writer, I remain dedicated to captivating my readers with evocative prose and insightful commentary. My commitment to my craft and my ability to connect with my audience make me a distinctive and cherished voice in contemporary literature.

Thank you for taking the time to learn more about me and my journey as a writer. I am grateful for the support and encouragement of my readers, and I am excited to continue sharing stories that inspire, inform, and entertain. Whether you have been with me from the beginning or are discovering my work for the first time, I appreciate your interest and look forward to connecting with you through my writing.

MAGGIE SMITH: A LEGENDARY EXIT

The Final Curtain Call of Cinema's Unmatched Grande Dame, and the Legacy She Left Behind

Shirley R. Benz

Table of contents

Title Page
COPYRIGHT ©
Preface
ABOUT THE AUTHOR
INTRODUCTION
CHAPTER 1.
- Early Life and Family Background
- Finding Her Footing in Acting

CHAPTER 2.
- The Stage Queen
- Breaking into Film
- Balancing Theater and Cinema

CHAPTER 3.
- Hollywood and Beyond
- Character Mastery
- Critical Acclaim and Awards

CHAPTER 4.
- Becoming a Global Icon
- The Wit and Wisdom of Her Roles

- Behind the Scenes

CHAPTER 5.
- Age and Grace
- Her Reflections on Career and Life
- Her Decision to Step Back

CHAPTER 6.
- Her Death
- The Impact of Her Passing
- Public Tributes

CHAPTER 7.
- Her Place in Cinema and Theater History
- Generational Impact

CHAPTER 8.
- Off-Screen Persona
- Quiet Humanitarian

CHAPTER 9.
- Professor McGonagall
- The Dowager Countess
- Jean Brodie and Other Classics

CHAPTER 10.
- The Final Farewell
- Her Continuing Legacy

APPENDIX

- ❖ Filmography
- ❖ Awards and Accolades
- ❖ Quotes by Maggie Smith

INTRODUCTION

In the domain of theater and television, few names reverberate as strongly as that of Dame Maggie Smith. Her legacy surpasses ordinary acting she was a force of nature, a master of her profession whose talent affected generations. To those who marveled at her acerbic wit as the Dowager Countess on Downton Abbey or found solace in the stern yet kind presence of Professor McGonagall in Harry Potter, Maggie was more than a performer; she was a constant, a reminder of excellence, persistence, and the timeless power of storytelling. She inhabited every role with an elegance few could ever aspire to.

But beneath the brilliant limelight, above the plaudits and trophies, there was something genuinely human about Maggie Smith. Born in 1934, she went on a journey that lasted six decades, navigating not just the ebbs and flows of an ever-evolving entertainment scene but also the fundamental fabric of human existence. She gave voice to women who were feisty, imperfect, and unflinchingly honest, providing viewers with characters who stayed long after the curtains dropped.

The day she departed September 27, 2024, marked more than the death of a famous actress. It was the end of an era. An outpouring of sadness, admiration, and affection surged around the world, from theatrical fans in London to Hollywood celebrities in Los Angeles. Yet among the pain, there was a common recognition: Maggie Smith's legacy was permanent. Her last curtain call, although received with grief, was also a celebration of a life lived completely and a career that established an unsurpassed standard.

In this biography, we dig into the life of a woman who, through her ability and persistence, transformed not just the parts she portrayed but the lives of those who watched her. As we follow her path from the dusty stages of Oxford Playhouse to her dominating presence in worldwide blockbuster franchises, we examine not only her professional highlights but the quiet resilience and burning determination that characterized Maggie Smith the person.

This is not simply a tale of an actress it is the story of a legend. The world mourns her departure, but her brilliance lingers, eternally blazing the road for performers, artists, and visionaries. This is Maggie Smith's last bow, her iconic farewell.

CHAPTER 1.

Beginnings of a Star

(1934–1950s)

Early Life and Family Background

Maggie Smith was born on December 28, 1934, in Ilford, Essex, England. At the time, no one could have expected that this kid, born to a modest family, would grow to become one of the most famous and renowned names in cinema and theater. Her upbringing, albeit not drenched in the spotlight from birth, had a significant part in developing her as an artist who would eventually grab the world's hearts with her spectacular performances.

Her father, Nathaniel Smith, was a pathologist at the University of Oxford, while her mother, Margaret Hutton Little, originated from Glasgow, Scotland. Though her father's career kept him completely involved with his medical practice, it was her mother who fostered Maggie's artistic energy. Margaret, herself a devotee of the arts, saw early on that her daughter had a special spark. Though not a stagemother by any means, she encouraged Maggie to explore the world of performing, allowing her the opportunity to follow her natural inclinations. The confluence of academic rigor from her father's side and the artistic tendency of her mother presented Maggie with a unique balance one that would later make her a performer of intellectual depth and emotional breadth.

Maggie's upbringing was not without its obstacles. The advent of World Conflict II influenced her formative years, and like many youngsters of her day, she observed her family experience difficulties brought on by the conflict. Her father's employment at Oxford meant the family relocated to the city when she was young. It was here, among the shadows of academic institutions and amidst the clamor of a changing world, that Maggie first started to find her passion for performing.

Her exposure to the arts was casual yet powerful. As a young kid, Maggie found herself intrigued by cinema, theater, and storytelling. The cinema was not simply an escape; it was a doorway to other realms, a place where she could immerse herself in the performances of the silver screen's best performers. It didn't take long for her to discover that her heartbeat for the stage. By the age of 16, Maggie's passion for acting had turned into something considerably more serious.

Finding Her Footing in Acting

Maggie's schooling was just as transforming as her creative leanings. She attended Oxford High School for Girls, where her curiosity was stimulated by literature and the performing arts. Despite her inherent affinity for acting, her road to the theater wasn't a simple or straight one. Acting as a career wasn't frequently supported in those days, and the young Maggie faced misgivings from society as well as from her own family. Nevertheless, her mother continued to silently encourage her dreams, seeing a gift that would not be simply faded.

Her major break came when she joined the Oxford Playhouse, a choice that marked the beginning of her famous career. The Oxford Playhouse, a notable local theater with a long-standing reputation for developing raw talent, became her training ground. It was here that she would refine her craft, learning the complexities of acting, timing, and the emotional sensitivity necessary to properly enter a part. Her initial jobs were small, and while she wasn't yet the Maggie Smith the world would come to know, she was already displaying flashes of the brilliance that would characterize her career. Her professors and mentors at the Playhouse were instantly captivated by her raw ability and unrelenting effort.

During this age, Maggie's inherent wit and sharpness of intellect set her apart. The stage was not merely a platform for expression but a location where her intellect could come through. Even in those early days, spectators noticed her unique ability to mix comedy with solemnity, something that would become a characteristic of her performances in later years.

The 1950s were a key moment for Maggie. While many of her contemporaries struggled to establish their feet, she started to carve out a space for herself. Her fame expanded with each part, as she exhibited incredible versatility and a knack for both tragic and humorous performances. As part of the post-war generation of performers, she accepted a theatrical world that was starting to transform, with new forms and topics developing in the aftermath of global turmoil.

Though her early work was mostly on stage, Maggie started to garner notice from individuals in the film business. Her transfer from theater to cinema would take time, but the seeds were sown. As she reached her twenties, Maggie Smith was no longer simply a hopeful actor but a budding star on the British stage a young lady whose career was ready to take off.

The leap from Oxford Playhouse to bigger, more prominent venues came effortlessly to Maggie. She started to gain the attention of directors and producers, notably those at the Royal National Theatre. By the mid-1950s, her theatrical work had gained her a loyal following, with reviewers and spectators alike appreciating her performances for their intricacy, comedy, and emotional depth.

It was in these early years that the world started to witness the birth of Maggie Smith we today celebrate a lady of enormous skill and intelligence, with an unrivaled capacity to embody characters in a manner that seemed both profoundly personal and widely sympathetic. Her path from a little child in Essex to an ambitious actor at Oxford Playhouse created the groundwork for a career that would span more than six decades, making an unforgettable influence on the world of acting.

Maggie's early existence was marked by a calm resolve. She wasn't born into celebrity or luxury; rather, she established her reputation through effort, skill, and an uncompromising confidence in the power of narrative. As we continue through her journey, we'll discover how these formative years established the framework for the incredible career that followed, and how the events of her upbringing impacted the iconic roles she would later embark on.

CHAPTER 2.

Theater to Stardom

(1960s-1970s)

The Stage Queen

By the time the 1960s got around, Dame Maggie Smith had already started to establish herself as a force on the British stage, but it was during this decade that she firmly secured her place as one of the top theatrical talents of her generation. Her debut occurred under the supervision of Sir Laurence Olivier, one of the most revered characters in British theater. It was Olivier who spotted Maggie's enormous skill early on and persuaded her to join the newly created National Theatre in London, where she became a cornerstone of the company's productions.

Working under Olivier's supervision was a masterclass in the art of theatrical acting. Maggie's work at this period includes impressive performances in both classical and contemporary plays, spanning from Shakespeare to more current pieces. Her ability to move between the royal and the humorous, to express wit as well as profound melancholy, distinguished her as a rare talent. In performances like The Master Builder and Much Ado About Nothing, she astonished audiences with her quick delivery and emotional range, traits that would become her hallmarks.

It was this time that also distinguished Maggie Smith as a "Stage Queen" in her own right. Her regal posture, impeccable enunciation, and imposing presence on stage attracted parallels to royalty, a term she would eventually embody in more ways than one. But what actually set her apart from other actresses of the age was her ability to locate the humanity in every character she performed, putting life into parts that others would have considered as just intellectual. The National Theatre provided her a platform to explore the full spectrum of her gift, and under Olivier's careful eye, she blossomed.

One of the distinguishing features of this phase in Maggie's career was her constant pursuit of greatness. Even as she became one of the most sought-after actors in the theatrical industry, she never rested on her laurels. Instead, she continued to challenge herself with each new part, continuously pushing the limits of what she could do as a performer. Whether she was portraying a Shakespearean heroine or a character from a current drama, Maggie always brought a freshness and vigor to the stage that grabbed viewers.

Her theatrical supremacy throughout the 1960s established her as an important figure in British theater. The framework she set in these years would have a lasting influence on her career, showing that she could flourish in a medium that needed the greatest degree of ability and devotion. For Maggie Smith, the theater was where her star first started to shine, and it was a platform she would never completely leave behind, even as her career moved into other fields.

Breaking into Film

While the stage was where Maggie Smith originally achieved notoriety, it was her flawless move into cinema that converted her from a British theatrical wonder into a worldwide celebrity. As she transitioned from theater to film, her acting talent continued to shine, and the 1960s and 1970s were an era of stratospheric ascent for Maggie in the world of cinema.

Her breakout performance in The Prime of Miss Jean Brodie (1969) was nothing short of legendary. Maggie's depiction of the unusual and controversial schoolteacher gained her global praise and established her as a cinematic star in her own right. Jean Brodie was a figure of depth and contradiction a lady full of charm, intellect, and passion but also one who held dangerous political sentiments and was oblivious to the implications of her actions. Maggie's ability to convey both the charm and the inherent defects of Miss Brodie was nothing short of astounding, and it won her the Academy Award for Best Actress. This part not only highlighted Maggie's incredible versatility but also sealed her reputation as an actress who could command the cinema as well as the stage.

Following the triumph of The Prime of Miss Jean Brodie, Maggie proceeded to make her mark in film with a run of remarkable performances. One of the most notable was her appearance in California Suite (1978), a picture that once again showcased her flexibility as an actor. In this Neil Simon comedy, Maggie portrayed an actress nominated for an Academy Award, echoing her real-life triumphs. The part was both humorous and sad, and Maggie's ability to manage the emotional highs and lows of the character won her a second Academy Award, this time for Best Supporting Actress.

Throughout the 1970s, Maggie's work in films demonstrated an uncommon blend of seriousness and comedy. She flowed seamlessly between drama and humor, revealing herself to be a multidimensional actor who could flourish in any genre. Her work in this era showcased her ability to impart complexity and depth to even the most ostensibly basic characters. Whether she was portraying a no-nonsense schoolteacher or a torn actress, Maggie always found ways to make her roles seem genuine and approachable.

What made Maggie's accomplishment in cinema even more surprising was her ability to transmit the passion and discipline of her theatrical performance to the screen. Many stage actresses struggle to adjust to the demands of cinema, where delicacy and restraint are typically necessary, but Maggie had no such issue. Her performances in cinema were as forceful and authoritative as they were on stage, and it wasn't long before she became a staple in both the British and foreign film industries.

Balancing Theater and Cinema

Despite her burgeoning success in the film business, Maggie Smith never abandoned the stage. Instead, she became one of the few actresses who could shift smoothly between theater and film, excelling in both disciplines. The 1960s and 1970s were a period when Maggie successfully negotiated the demands of both her film career and her theatrical work, demonstrating again and again that she was a master of both disciplines.

One of the secrets to Maggie's success in combining these two demanding occupations was her uncompromising devotion to her work. She handled every part whether on stage or television with the same degree of devotion and preparation. While many performers would have found it difficult to combine the physicality of theater with the more personal demands of cinema, Maggie appeared to flourish in both contexts. In fact, it was commonly stated that her theater performances impacted her cinema work and vice versa. The emotional intensity she brought to the stage lent depth to her film parts, while the nuances she gained from film acting boosted her theatrical performances.

The 1970s saw Maggie continue her work with the National Theatre while concurrently expanding her cinematic career. During this era, she starred in shows such as The Merchant of Venice and The Three Sisters, where she once again enthralled audiences with her powerful performances. Even as her film appearances brought her worldwide renown, she remained a cherished character in the British theatrical industry.

Her ability to juggle these two hard occupations wasn't simply a credit to her skill it also represented her great passion for the art of acting. For Maggie, acting wasn't simply a job; it was a calling. Whether she was acting in front of a camera or an audience, she brought the same passion and intensity to every part. It was this constant focus that enabled her to accomplish what so few actresses achieved in both the realms of theater and cinema.

By the end of the 1970s, Maggie Smith had firmly established herself as one of the most varied and acclaimed actors of her period. Her ability to flourish in both theater and cinema set her apart from her classmates, and it was evident that there was no role too tough or medium too demanding for Maggie. As she prepared to start the next part of her career, it was apparent that her popularity would continue to climb, both on the stage and in the cinema.

Maggie Smith's path throughout the 1960s and 1970s was one of amazing development and progress. From her ascent to popularity on the stage to her breakthrough in cinema, she mastered the challenges of both genres with elegance and drive. This phase of her life created the framework for the incredible career that would follow, as she proceeded to fascinate audiences throughout the globe with her unique skill.

CHAPTER 3.

A Filmography of Excellence

(1980s–1990s)

Hollywood and Beyond

Maggie Smith's journey into the Hollywood limelight in the 1980s represented a key juncture in her brilliant career. She was no longer merely a beloved British theater and screen actress; she was now entering the world of international celebrity, drawing viewers outside the UK. By this time, Maggie had already earned a name for herself with her remarkable work in cinema and on stage. Yet, it was her foray into Hollywood, with parts that displayed her variety and depth, that really sealed her image as a worldwide legend.

The 1985 film A Room with a View, directed by James Ivory, was one of the important movies that brought Maggie Smith to Hollywood in a big fashion. Playing the part of Charlotte Bartlett, a character replete with primness and controlled emotions, Maggie exhibited her unrivaled ability to communicate layers of personality with subtlety. In many respects, this performance epitomized Maggie's aptitude for portraying strong-willed women with complicated emotional undercurrents. A Room with a View was a financial success and critically lauded, gaining numerous Academy Award nominations, including one for Maggie herself in the category of Best Supporting Actress.

In 1987, Smith once again demonstrated her genius in The Lonely Passion of Judith Hearne, where she portrayed the title character, a lonely, middle-aged woman dealing with her waning aspirations for love and the growing sorrow of a life unfulfilled. This part was possibly one of Maggie's most demanding, since it needed her to dive into the deep psychological components of her character, displaying both fragility and strength. Judith Hearne was an extremely difficult picture, and Maggie's depiction of the character gained her tremendous acclaim, further establishing her status in both Hollywood and foreign cinema.

Throughout the late 1980s, Smith continued to mix her employment between Hollywood blockbusters and British projects. She became noted for her ability to transition smoothly between diverse genres, showing herself equally capable of producing affecting performances in both serious and humorous parts. This balance guaranteed that Maggie remained a flexible actor, never bound to a specific sort of character or environment.

Character Mastery

If there was one feature of Maggie Smith's career that marked her apart from her peers, it was her unrivaled ability to brilliantly portray a broad array of roles. From the aristocratic to the destitute, from the wonderfully sharp-tongued to the tragically heartbreaking, Maggie was a genuine chameleon on film. The late 1980s and early 1990s were a time of character discovery and mastery for her, as she took on parts that enabled her to completely exhibit her versatility as an actor.

One of the distinctive qualities of Maggie's characters during this period was her depiction of smart, sharp-tongued ladies, a repeating motif in many of her appearances. In films like A Room with a View and The Prime of Miss Jean Brodie (while released earlier in her career, its repercussions lingered into her subsequent roles), Maggie inhabited characters who typically emanated authority, but were tinged with comedy, wit, and, at times, a touch of sadness. She became noted for her caustic humor, delivered with exquisite timing, but always underpinned with a vulnerability that made her characters truly real.

Maggie's ability to inhabit dramatically diverse parts didn't simply arise from her inherent skill but was also a consequence of her focused dedication to the trade of acting. She notoriously spent hours analyzing her characters, diving deep into their motives and backstories, even when they weren't expressly mentioned in the screenplay. This commitment gave her performances a depth that few could equal. Whether she was portraying a spinster, a duchess, or a schoolmistress, Maggie Smith had the unusual capacity to make spectators believe in the reality of any role she inhabited.

Her depiction of powerful women in this era gave her a role model for actors, young and old, who desired to take on equally challenging parts. In a period when many female performers were pigeonholed into conventional roles, Maggie's career was evidence that women could portray a broad spectrum of characters, from the vulnerable to the formidable. This adaptability became a characteristic of her acting technique, and it further confirmed her as one of the most acclaimed actors of her time.

Critical Acclaim and Awards

Maggie Smith's performances throughout the 1980s and 1990s didn't simply fascinate audiences they also garnered her a series of important prizes. Her ability to pour life into people, no matter how great or tiny the part, made her a favorite with reviewers and award committees alike. Over the course of nearly two decades, Maggie garnered countless honors, each a testimonial to her ongoing talent as an actor.

In 1986, Maggie received the BAFTA Award for Best Actress in a Supporting Role for her depiction of Charlotte Bartlett in A Room with a View. This portrayal, which had already gained her tremendous recognition, was acknowledged as one of the best performances of the year. Her BAFTA triumph was followed by nominations at the Golden Globes and the Academy Awards, marking the start of a succession of award nominations that would become practically normal for Maggie in the following years.

One of her most highly lauded portrayals occurred in 1987 with The Lonely Passion of Judith Hearne. For her role in this picture, Maggie earned the Best Actress Award at the Evening Standard British Picture Awards, adding to her expanding collection of awards. This portrayal also got her a nomination for the BAFTA Award for Best Actress in a Leading portrayal, as well as nominations at other important award events across the globe.

Throughout the 1990s, Maggie continued to rack up accolades and awards for her efforts in cinema and television. In 1993, she earned the Golden Globe Award for Best Supporting Actress for her part in The Secret Garden, in which she portrayed the severe but compassionate Mrs. Medlock. This film further demonstrated her ability to impart depth and empathy to parts that may easily have been depicted as one-dimensional.

Maggie Smith's accolades were not merely a recognition of her brilliance but were also a testimonial to her durability and relevancy in an industry that is sometimes quick to ignore seasoned actresses. She became one of the rare actors who managed to remain at the top of their game for decades, continually improving and adapting to the ever-changing world of cinema and television.

By the end of the 1990s, Maggie Smith had firmly established herself as a legend in the world of film. Her prizes and accolades were many, but they were simply a reflection of the broader influence she had on the world of acting. With every job, she continued to lift the bar, setting a level for perfection that few could ever aspire to achieve. The world had come to expect greatness from Maggie, and time and time again, she delivered.

Maggie Smith's path throughout the 1980s and 1990s was one of creative progress and achievement. From her dominating presence in Hollywood to her understanding of complicated characters, she remained a force to be reckoned with, continuing to gain the affection of fans and critics alike. Through every character she portrayed, Maggie made an unforgettable stamp on the world of film, proving that great talent never fades it only becomes stronger with time.

CHAPTER 4.

The Dowager Countess and Hogwarts (2000s)

Becoming a Global Icon

Maggie Smith's work in the 2000s reinforced her standing as a real worldwide icon, partly owing to her depiction of two remarkable characters: the sharp-witted Dowager Countess of Downton Abbey and the powerful Professor Minerva McGonagall in the Harry Potter film trilogy. These roles enabled her to reach new generations of admirers and exhibit her extraordinary ability to breathe life into characters that made an enduring influence on pop culture.

The Dowager Countess of Grantham from Downton Abbey immediately became one of Maggie Smith's most admired performances. Premiering in 2010, Downton Abbey was an epic historical drama following the lives of the wealthy Crawley family and their servants in the early 20th century. Maggie, as the family matriarch, was a wonderful match for the series' themes of transition, class, and perseverance. The Dowager Countess, with her razor-sharp wit and no-nonsense attitude, was both feared and admired, and Maggie's depiction was nothing short of legendary. She gave depth and comedy to the part, with every line delivered with exquisite timing. Her Dowager Countess became a meme-worthy persona, and her performance resonated with fans well beyond the UK.

Simultaneously, Maggie was captivating an entirely other audience as Professor McGonagall in the Harry Potter flicks. Beginning in 2001 with Harry Potter and the Philosopher's Stone, Maggie's depiction of the no-nonsense Transfiguration instructor and deputy headmistress became famous. For a whole generation of viewers, she was McGonagall, representing the character's power, knowledge, and profound compassion for her pupils. The Harry Potter books became a worldwide sensation, and Maggie's presence in the films was a soothing and uplifting force. Her delivery of crucial phrases especially in times of seriousness nailed the spirit of J.K. Rowling's cherished heroine.

In both Downton Abbey and Harry Potter, Maggie found herself at the center of some of the most culturally important projects of the 2000s, and her impact stretched well beyond the characters she portrayed. Her work in these series contributed considerably to their popularity, increasing the level of narrative with her remarkable expertise.

The Wit and Wisdom of Her Roles

It wasn't only the characters themselves that solidified Maggie Smith's fame in the 2000s it was her ability to infuse them with humor and wisdom, making them not just distinctive but also adored. The Dowager Countess of Downton Abbey became famed for her stinging one-liners, frequently disarming both characters and spectators with her sharp humor. Her lines like "What is a weekend?" became immediate classics, illustrating her character's deep-rooted aristocratic tastes, while also demonstrating her superb comic timing. Maggie's excellent delivery of such lines made them classic moments of the series, establishing her standing as a living legend in the entertainment business.

Professor McGonagall, on the other hand, gave a different type of knowledge. In the Harry Potter books, McGonagall was a figure of discipline, knowledge, and caring, attributes that Maggie represented with composure. Though less amusing than the Dowager Countess, McGonagall's moments of dry humor such as her deliciously biting "I've always wanted to use that spell" after leading Hogwarts' suits of armor into combat enthralled audiences. Moreover, Maggie endowed McGonagall with an underlying warmth, ensuring the character remained a beloved and soothing presence throughout the series. The seriousness of situations like as her defense of Harry, Hermione, and Ron before Dolores Umbridge brought levels of devotion and moral courage to her depiction, making her performances memorable.

Through these personalities, Maggie connected with viewers on numerous levels. Both the Dowager Countess and McGonagall were icons of authority and wisdom, but they were also sympathetic because of the comedy and humanity Maggie gave to them. These roles were a tribute to her exceptional ability to pull laughter and tears from her audience, demonstrating once again that she was a master of her art.

Behind the Scenes

Maggie Smith's depiction of these legendary characters wasn't simply adored by fans; her co-stars and colleagues also had the highest respect for her skill and work ethic. Despite overcoming personal obstacles such as a breast cancer diagnosis in 2008 Maggie stayed consistent in her devotion to her job, and her professionalism never faltered, even throughout tough production schedules.

On the set of Downton Abbey, Maggie's presence was regarded as both awe-inspiring and grounded. Co-stars have described how she could move from calm contemplation to delivering a hilarious line with flawless accuracy, leaving the whole cast in stitches. Michelle Dockery, who portrayed Lady Mary Crawley, previously remarked that working with Maggie was a lesson in acting. She told of how Maggie could dominate a room with a single look or pause, her grasp of timing unequaled.

Similarly, during her time on the Harry Potter sets, Maggie had a lasting influence on the younger cast members. Daniel Radcliffe, who portrayed Harry Potter, frequently stated how Maggie served as both an inspiration and a mentor. Despite the enormity of the production and the young energy around her, Maggie stayed focused, providing a degree of solemnity to her performances that grounded the magical aspects of the movie. Her performance of Professor McGonagall was one of the fundamental reasons the Harry Potter films kept their emotional depth, even amongst the magic and spectacle.

There are also beautiful anecdotes of Maggie's encounters with the actors and crew that demonstrate her sense of humor and modesty. Even as she became a worldwide figure, Maggie never took herself too seriously. On one occasion, after a particularly frigid day of shooting for Downton Abbey, she allegedly remarked, "Who do I have to kill to get a cup of tea around here?" Her quick wit and charm made her appreciated not only by fans but also by those who had the opportunity to work with her.

Maggie's devotion to her job, especially during tough personal moments, further endeared her to her coworkers. Her professionalism and perseverance were respected by many, and her performances throughout the 2000s are regarded as some of the greatest in her already brilliant career. Whether she was delivering a stinging response as the Dowager Countess or imparting words of wisdom as Professor McGonagall, Maggie's performances established a lasting legacy that will continue to inspire future generations of artists and spectators alike.

As the 2000s proceeded, Maggie Smith's performances in Downton Abbey and Harry Potter not only contributed to her already sparkling career but also reintroduced her to worldwide audiences. These two famous parts showed everything that made Maggie a once-in-a-generation talent: her humor, wisdom, and uncompromising devotion to her profession. Through her work, Maggie crossed media, decades, and genres, becoming an icon in both popular culture and the field of acting. Her performances throughout this era remain touchstones of quality, reminding us of her exceptional ability to embody any role with elegance, comedy, and depth.

CHAPTER 5.

The Final Act

(2010s-2024)

Age and Grace

Maggie Smith's career, which had already lasted more than six decades, continued to thrive well into her 80s. Age never slowed her down; in fact, it appeared to heighten the elegance and seriousness she gave to every performance. In the 2010s, she reinvented what it meant to mature as a performer in an industry that generally overlooks older women. She did not fade away quietly but instead picked jobs that represented both the wisdom and sharpness of her years.

After consolidating her worldwide stardom with Downton Abbey and Harry Potter, she became a lasting personality on both the stage and cinema. In 2015, Maggie reprised her role as the Dowager Countess for the Downton Abbey film, which was hailed with worldwide praise. Despite being far into her 80s, Maggie demonstrated the same wit and zest that had made the Dowager Countess one of television's most popular characters. Her command of acting enabled her to cross humor and drama seamlessly, reminding viewers that age is no limit to creative ability.

In this final period of her career, Maggie embraced her reputation as a cultural icon, playing in smaller, character-driven parts that emphasized her tremendous versatility. In films like The Lady in the Van (2015), where she portrayed a homeless lady who sleeps in the driveway of a British writer, Maggie reminded the world of her ability to perfectly mix comedy with tragedy. The film was a critical hit, and Maggie's depiction was acclaimed as one of her most genuinely human performances, distinguishing her as an actress still at the height of her talents.

Her ability to command attention on film remained unsurpassed, whether via her keen comic timing or her ability to deliver emotionally touching speeches. Even as she matured, Maggie continued to grow as an actor, refusing to be typecast or constrained by her years. She continued working, and each job added more dimensions to her already renowned career.

Her Reflections on Career and Life

Maggie Smith has always been renowned as a quiet lady, but in her final years, she provided insights into her musings on life, profession, and aging. In multiple interviews, she talked openly about her relationship with acting, stardom, and how it felt to grow older in a profession obsessed with youth. Unlike many of her contemporaries, Maggie appeared to embrace the aging process with dignity and elegance, displaying a profound knowledge that time ultimately catches up with everyone.

One of the most remarkable elements of her interviews was her humility. Despite her numerous accolades including two Academy Awards, five BAFTAs, and a Tony Award Maggie generally minimized her accomplishments. She once famously quipped, "I'm just doing my job," a comment that summed up her no-nonsense attitude to acting and life. She never sought the limelight for the sake of notoriety, and maybe that's why she remained such a revered figure throughout her career.

In her final years, Maggie talked frequently about the toll aging takes, both physically and mentally. "I feel quite ancient," she said in a 2019 interview. She was upfront about her issues with health, having fought breast cancer in the 2000s, but she never allowed these obstacles to define her. In describing her performance in The Lady in the Van, she reminisced, "I was a bit tired, but I thought it was a good idea to get up and do something." This phrase describes Maggie's unrelenting attitude, even as the years slipped by. She embraced age with elegance, but she never let it stop her from doing what she loved.

Beyond performing, Maggie's ideas on fame were similarly illuminating. In a society increasingly driven by social media and rapid satisfaction, she stayed refreshingly free from the trappings of notoriety. Fame, to her, was merely a result of a life spent refining her profession. "I don't like it," she once declared of celebrity, "and I've never sought it out." Her connection with acting was one of genuine appreciation for the art form itself, not for the recognition it earned.

In this stage of life, Maggie also started pondering her career's influence and the legacy she would leave behind. Yet, even while celebrating her triumphs, there remained a lightness in her tone. She frequently said that she was shocked by the duration of her career, and never expected to still be working in her 80s. However, her performances continued to leave an indelible impact, guaranteeing that she would be hailed as one of the best performers of her time.

Her Decision to Step Back

As the years went on, it became evident that Maggie Smith was beginning to progressively recede from public life. Though she stayed involved in the business until her late 80s, her appearances grew fewer, and it was apparent that she was eager to step back and live a simpler life. After ending her work on the Downton Abbey movie and The Lady in the Van, she featured in fewer productions, focusing on more chosen parts. This steady retreat from the spotlight was in line with her personality; Maggie had never desired attention and was willing to let her body of work speak for itself.

By the early 2020s, Maggie had all but retired from performing. Her final significant performance was in A Boy Called Christmas (2021), when she once again brought warmth and humor to the screen. After this, her public appearances were reduced. Fans wondered about her health, but Maggie, as usual, remained discreet, admitting only a select few inside her personal life. There was no spectacular goodbye, no public proclamation of retirement just a gentle fading off the screen.

Yet, even as she stood aside, the world continued to appreciate her achievements. She won lifetime achievement awards, and her legacy was preserved in innumerable retrospectives, essays, and interviews. Her retirement, much like her career, was defined by elegance and humility. Maggie had given the world decades of spectacular performances, and now, she was glad to relax and reflect on a life well-lived.

Maggie Smith's last act was one of calm strength and deep introspection. Even as she aged, she remained a towering presence in the world of acting, liked by fans and revered by her colleagues. Her choice to step back from acting was not a retreat but a logical evolution for an actress who had already contributed so much. She left behind a legacy of greatness, a tribute to the force of passion, determination, and an unshakable devotion to her profession.

As Maggie herself once observed, "I've had a wonderful career. Now it's time to enjoy the peace." And in her latter years, she did exactly that, knowing that her work would continue to inspire generations to come.

CHAPTER 6.

The Day the Curtains Closed

(September 27, 2024)

Her Death

On the morning of September 27, 2024, the world awakened to the terrible news that Dame Maggie Smith had gone away at the age of 89. Her death was a peaceful and dignified farewell, much like the lady herself. She had been battling with health issues, but her family, ever protective of her privacy, had not publicly addressed the facts of her ailment. Surrounded by her loved ones, Maggie took her last bow in the comfort of her home in the English countryside.

The statement from her family expressed the feeling of veneration that everyone felt for her: "It is with tremendous regret that we announce the demise of Dame Maggie Smith. She was a loving mother, grandmother, and one of the best performers of her time. We beg for privacy at this tough period."

The demise of Maggie Smith rippled across the entertainment business. From her early days in British theater to her worldwide popularity in Downton Abbey and the Harry Potter series, her death signaled the end of an era. Her coworkers, admirers, and others who had the opportunity of working with her shared tributes that testified to her compassion, intellect, and continuing effect. Fellow performers from both theater and film sent touching remarks on social media, recognizing not just her enormous skill but also her humor, generosity, and humility.

The Impact of Her Passing

The first reaction to Maggie Smith's death was one of tremendous grief. Her demise was more than simply the loss of a brilliant actor; it was the closure of a chapter in the history of British and world film. In a world that had grown to depend on her performances for both comfort and inspiration, the loss seemed personal for millions of followers.

In the days after the announcement, notable personalities from all corners of the entertainment world recounted recollections of working with Dame Maggie. Emma Thompson, who appeared alongside her in Harry Potter and on Broadway, observed, "She was matchless. There was no one like her and there never will be." Other performers and directors shared this view, recognizing her effect on their careers and the larger industry. From directors to costume designers, Maggie Smith has impacted many lives, all of whom testified of her persistent work ethic, acute wit, and unrivaled presence on stage and television.

Her death was not merely mourned by those in the profession. Fans across the globe sent personal condolences, remembering the instances her performances had affected them, inspired them, or just made them laugh. For many, Maggie was a staple of their cultural landscape, whether as the ferociously witty Dowager Countess of Downton Abbey or the stern but compassionate Professor McGonagall in Harry Potter. In every part, she provided a humanity that transcended the screen, making her demise a keenly felt loss for everybody.

Public Tributes

The world reacted with a succession of public tributes recognizing Maggie Smith's outstanding career and legacy. One of the first came from the crew behind Downton Abbey, where she had notably played the Dowager Countess. Julian Fellowes, creator of the series, led the homage, stating, "Maggie Smith was the heart and soul of Downton Abbey. Her depiction of Violet Crawley will go down as one of the finest performances in television history. We are grieved by her departure and will forever be in her debt for the pleasure she brought to our screens." The cast of the series united in a memorial ceremony arranged to celebrate Maggie's life, where her most memorable sequences from the series were displayed, reminding the audience of the humor, charm, and compassion she gave to her role.

Similarly, the Harry Potter series paid its homage. A special tribute from J.K. Rowling said, "Maggie was the essence of

Professor McGonagall, a figure who, like her, was filled with integrity, knowledge, and strength. I shall eternally be thankful for her contribution to the enchantment of Harry Potter." The Harry Potter cast also created a virtual homage, where they offered behind-the-scenes anecdotes and personal experiences of working with her, stressing not just her brilliance but her mentoring to younger performers, who regarded her as a guiding figure throughout the films.

The National Theatre, where Maggie Smith had worked during her early years with Laurence Olivier, staged a touching commemoration of her theatrical career. It included performances of some of her most memorable roles, including The Importance of Being Earnest and Hedda Gabler, and a speech by Sir Ian McKellen, who had played with Maggie on countless times. "Maggie was the bedrock of British theater," McKellen stated. "She had an energy and brilliance that could fill any room, and every role she played was brought to life with unparalleled authenticity."

Across London's West End, marquees were lighted with inscriptions remembering her outstanding achievements to theater. Several theaters staged a minute's silence before their evening shows, remembering her as a cornerstone of British stagecraft.

Internationally, tributes flowed in as well. The Cannes Film Festival announced a unique retrospective of her career, showing a selection of her most recognized works. Critics and fans reacted on her ability to create emotionally complex performances, whether in historical plays or modern productions, making her a popular at film festivals throughout the globe.

Maggie Smith's demise was mourned widely, but the tributes also emphasized the enormous pleasure she had provided to millions of people. Her legacy, solidified by her tremendous collection of work, will live on for years to come. Fans, colleagues, and friends recognized that Maggie Smith was more than an actress she was a master of her trade, a legend whose effect would echo for years to come.

CHAPTER 7.

A Legacy Etched in Eternity

Her Place in Cinema and Theater History

When the last curtain dropped on Dame Maggie Smith's life, it wasn't only the conclusion of a spectacular career, but the completion of a journey that left an indelible impression on the world of performing arts. Her reputation, spanning over seven decades, will long be connected with greatness in acting. From the sophisticated halls of British theater to the broad realm of global film, Maggie carved out a spot where few performers ever accomplish a position at the very heart of dramatic history.

Smith's early years in theater, notably under the mentorship of Laurence Olivier at the National Theatre, served him to define a career that became renowned in its range and complexity. Her command over the stage, her exquisite timing, and her ability to turn from comedy to drama with ease won her the label of "Stage Queen" among reviewers and colleagues alike. It was this adaptability that transferred to her movie career, resulting in her legendary parts in films such as The Prime of Miss Jean Brodie and California Suite, which earned her two Academy Awards.

In many respects, Smith's work will be regarded as a bridge between the conventional theatrical world and contemporary cinema, with a filmography that reflects the growing character of both genres. Whether playing aristocratic matriarchs or powerful, funny women, she continually created performances that were engaging, complex, and ageless. Her name, indelibly inscribed into the annals of both film and theatrical history, will be spoken alongside other greats those whose talents transcended the periods in which they worked.

Generational Impact

What makes Maggie Smith's legacy even more amazing is her ability to transcend decades. Many of her contemporaries stayed adored by a certain audience, but Smith's work touched both older theatergoers and new followers. For those who grew up watching her on Downton Abbey and Harry Potter, Maggie was more than simply an actor she was a cultural phenomenon.

Her role as Professor McGonagall in the Harry Potter series exposed her to a new generation, with young viewers finding the same razor-sharp wit and compelling presence that had captivated audiences in the 1960s and 1970s. In Downton Abbey, Smith's character, the Dowager Countess, became a symbol of elegance, humor, and perseverance, offering some of the most famous quips and sequences in the series. Through these portrayals, Maggie Smith became a household name for a generation far away from her early work in British theater.

More significantly, she served as an inspiration to innumerable budding actresses. For young actors, in particular, Smith's career represented a pattern of durability, flexibility, and elegance. Many current actresses have acknowledged her as a role model, someone who showed the greatest degree of devotion to the trade. She demonstrated that age was never a barrier to talent, continuing to give award-winning performances far into her 80s. Smith proved that one might grow with the times without abandoning the integrity and depth that marked their craft.

What She Left Behind Dame Maggie Smith's enduring legacy is not simply the remarkable performances she gave but also the enormous contributions she made to the arts community as a whole. Over the course of her life, Smith garnered countless awards, including BAFTAs, Golden Globes, and Academy Awards, confirming her place as one of the best actors of her time. Yet, beyond the prizes and honors, Maggie's true legacy was the body of work she left behind work that would continue to inspire and enchant future generations.

Her effect wasn't restricted to the movie and stage. Off-screen, Maggie Smith was noted for her charity endeavors. She discreetly supported several organizations, notably those relating to cancer research, having survived breast cancer herself. Her passion for charity, while seldom publicized, revealed the depth of her character a lady who utilized her power to benefit the world around her.

Smith's enduring effect on the business stretches well beyond her jobs. She illustrated that success was not only about celebrity or wealth but about the love of the trade. Her work ethic, professionalism, and relentless quest for excellence served as an example for people in the entertainment business. Even after her demise, the tales she left behind, the characters she brought to life, and the passion she displayed for her craft continue to reverberate.

As the world looks at Maggie Smith's extraordinary life and career, it becomes evident that her legacy is not simply a chapter in the history of acting it is a cornerstone. She will be remembered not just for her remarkable skill but for the elegance, humor, and compassion she brought to every character she portrayed, leaving an enduring impression on both film and theater.

CHAPTER 8.

The Personal Side of Maggie Smith's Family Life

Behind the royal personas, keen humor, and world-renowned performances, Dame Maggie Smith's personal life was a gentler, more private narrative, founded on love, family, and perseverance. Born to Nathaniel Smith, a pathologist, and Margaret Hutton Little, a secretary, Maggie acquired a sense of discipline and humility, attributes that would assist her throughout her amazing career. Her childhood in Ilford, Essex, gave her a firm foundation of ideals that would affect her approach to both life and art.

Maggie married twice throughout her lifetime. Her first marriage, to actor Robert

Stephens in 1967, lasted until 1975. Together, they had two sons, both of whom followed in their parents' paths into the field of acting: Chris Larkin and Toby Stephens. Chris, famed for his work in British movies and television, has frequently been cast in military roles, while Toby acquired worldwide acclaim for his depiction as Captain Flint in Black Sails. Maggie's bond with her kids was a steady source of pride throughout her life, and her support for their vocations was unshakable.

In 1975, Maggie remarried, this time to writer Beverley Cross. It was a collaboration founded on mutual respect and artistic fire, one that provided her peace following the loss of her first marriage. Cross's sudden death in 1998 was a tremendous loss for Maggie, but even despite her own anguish, she continued to contribute to her audience with every part she took on. Though she stayed secretive about her personal sadness, her strength shined through as she poured her emotions into her art.

Off-Screen Persona

Despite being one of the most renowned actresses of her period, Maggie Smith was known for her humility and down-to-earth nature off-screen. Far from the larger-than-life characters she played, Maggie was frequently regarded as someone who cherished quiet and simplicity. Though she seldom gave interviews, those who worked closely with her recalled memories of her humor, modesty, and passion for her profession.

Colleagues have commented about her outstanding professionalism, characterizing her as someone who always came prepared, ready to work, and happy to mentor those around her. One of the most notable elements of her personality was her razor-sharp humor, which paralleled many of the roles she portrayed. While she tended to keep out of the limelight while not working, Maggie could be tremendously lively and loved cracking jokes with her fellow performers.

Even in her latter years, when she was generally recognized as an icon of British film, Maggie never took herself too seriously. Despite being honored with titles and accolades, she remained self-effacing, frequently poking fun at her position as a dame and at the expensive events she attended. While she did not want popularity, she accepted it with grace, preferring to concentrate on the profession of acting rather than the trappings of stardom.

Quiet Humanitarian

Maggie Smith's benevolence stretched beyond the theater and film. Though she wanted to keep her philanthropic activities quiet, people close to her knew that she supported a number of organizations, notably those relating to cancer research, having survived breast cancer herself in the late 1980s. Her experience with the sickness only heightened her sympathy for those going through similar challenges, and she silently gave to cancer organizations for many years.

Smith also utilized her influence to assist the arts, giving to organizations that encouraged fresh talent. As someone who had received mentoring from greats like Laurence Olivier, she was dedicated to ensuring that the next generation of performers had the same opportunity to study and progress within the business. Though she shied away from huge, public demonstrations of her giving, her gifts had a tremendous influence on both the arts and medical sectors.

Her humility in these endeavors matched her whole attitude to life. For Maggie, the most essential thing was to be loyal to herself, to her family, and to the principles she held dear. Fame was never something she desired, but rather a result of the passion she had for performing. Her humanitarian effort, like her profession, was done with honesty, elegance, and a feeling of duty toward others.

CHAPTER 9.

Maggie's Most Iconic Roles

(Deep Dive)

Professor McGonagall

When Harry Potter fans think of Professor Minerva McGonagall, the picture of Dame Maggie Smith automatically comes to mind. From the minute she initially appeared on-screen, donning her signature green robes and stern demeanor, it was evident that Smith had given something truly unique to this popular figure. McGonagall, the Transfiguration professor and Head of Gryffindor House at Hogwarts, became associated with intelligence, strength, and uncompromising loyalty a mirror of the traits Maggie herself exhibited both on and off the screen.

Smith's depiction was a lesson in restraint. Though McGonagall might have easily been presented as a one-dimensional authoritative figure, Maggie injected her with a gentle warmth and a sense of humor that gently simmered under her harsh persona. Her sharp, no-nonsense attitude and quick wit become one of the highlights of the Harry Potter series, as proven by her numerous quotable remarks. Fans notably remember her dominating presence in Harry Potter and the Deathly Hallows: Part 2, when her leadership in the Battle of Hogwarts and her unforgettable moment with the Piertotum Locomotor spell became legendary.

Maggie previously said that, despite the health challenges she had during shooting the last Harry Potter movies she fought breast cancer throughout production she was determined to complete the part, as she didn't want to let the audience down. This further increased to her position as a hero, both to her coworkers and to millions of Potter fans across the globe. McGonagall became a symbol of strength and guidance, and Maggie's commitment to the job assured that it would survive for centuries.

The Dowager Countess

If there's a single performance that sparked Maggie Smith's renown throughout the world in her latter years, it was her depiction as the tenacious Violet Crawley, Dowager Countess of Grantham, in Downton Abbey. Maggie's portrayal in this British historical drama was nothing short of fascinating, depicting a sharp-tongued, aristocratic matriarch whose stinging barbs and surprising flashes of sympathy made her an audience favorite.

The part of the Dowager Countess appeared to be designed just for Maggie, and she inhabited the character with an ease that was both captivating and amusing. Her humor formed the heart of Downton Abbey, with phrases like "What is a weekend?" and "Vulgarity is no substitute for wit," becoming immediate classics. Her subtle acting added dimension to a character who might have easily been written off as just a source of comedic relief. Violet was much more than that she was passionately devoted to her family, a guardian of tradition, and yet, capable of shocking vulnerability, frequently hidden behind her fast retorts and sharp wit.

The relationship with the fellow actresses, notably Penelope Wilton (who portrayed Isobel Crawley), enhanced to the charm. Their constant battle of wills created some of the show's most amusing moments. Maggie earned several prizes for her depiction, including three Primetime Emmy prizes, establishing her position in television history. The Dowager Countess, with her combination of wisdom, elegance, and caustic humor, established an archetype that future generations would remember, once again confirming Maggie's extraordinary ability to leave an everlasting stamp on every part she touched.

Jean Brodie and Other Classics

Long before she became recognized as Professor McGonagall or the Dowager Countess, Maggie Smith had already established herself as a tour de force in film. Among her most recognized parts was Jean Brodie in The Prime of Miss Jean Brodie (1969). The performance, which earned her an Academy Award for Best Actress, was nothing short of spectacular. As Jean Brodie, Maggie depicted an eccentric and idealistic schoolteacher whose idealized perspective of life and fascist sympathies eventually led to catastrophe.

Jean Brodie was one of those rare parts that needed an actor to manage the intricacies of a character who was both charming and tragically damaged. Maggie brilliantly negotiated that edge, producing a performance that was as compelling as it was terrifying. The profundity of her portrayal meant that spectators and reviewers alike could not turn away, despite Brodie's increasingly destructive actions. It was a career-defining performance that established Maggie Smith as one of the best actors of her age.

Other memorable parts include her portrayal in California Suite (1978), for which she earned her second Academy Award, this time for Best Supporting Actress. In the film, Maggie portrayed an actress on the edge of losing her husband while attending the Academy Awards, an ironic twist that displayed her talent to depict individuals battling with inner vulnerability under a polished façade. Her ability to communicate fragility and power in equal measure became her signature, and her performances still stand as milestones in the history of film.

From The Prime of Miss Jean Brodie to California Suite, Maggie's work in cinema revealed her incredible variety. She could depict severely flawed people with heart and sympathy, bringing viewers into their inner conflicts. These roles, albeit decades old, remain ageless in their emotional impact, reminding us why Maggie Smith will always be recognized as one of the greats.

CHAPTER 10.

Saying Goodbye

The Final Farewell

When the world learned of Dame Maggie Smith's demise, the worldwide entertainment community replied with a wave of tributes that showed great affection for her seven-decade-long career. In the days after her death, memorials and tributes were organized across numerous platforms both official ceremonies and sincere public celebrations of her life. Fans flocked outside theaters where Maggie had played, leaving flowers, messages, and keepsakes in tribute to the great actress who had been a part of their lives for so many years.

In London's West End, where her career started, theaters lowered their lights in a mournful homage. The National Theatre, where she had done so many legendary parts under the guidance of Laurence Olivier, prepared a retrospective evening devoted to her achievements in the theater, with performances by performers who had shared the stage with her over the decades. Their tales demonstrated not just her talent but also her compassion, humility, and commitment to her work. In Hollywood, prominent movie groups paid homage with special showings of her films, ranging from The Prime of Miss Jean Brodie to Harry Potter, demonstrating the breadth of her oeuvre.

Fans of Downton Abbey and Harry Potter also lost her intensely, with fan gatherings turning into sites for communal commemoration. Downton Abbey planned a special tribute with the cast and crew to remember the character of Violet Crawley, a role that had revived Maggie's renown worldwide. The creators of Harry Potter similarly honored her during a commemorative gathering, with other cast members noting the knowledge, humor, and kindness that Maggie gave to the set, both on- and off-camera. One could feel the enormous influence she had not just as an actor but as a mentor and friend.

Her Continuing Legacy

Even though the curtains have fallen on Dame Maggie Smith's life, her legacy will continue to flourish in ways few actresses could ever conceive. In the same manner that her characters have etched themselves into the hearts of viewers, Maggie herself has made an everlasting impression on the entertainment business.

Her collection of work will be studied by future generations of performers who aspire to the same elegance, humor, and range that Maggie brought to her parts. Acting schools throughout the world now feature her performances as Professor McGonagall, Violet Crawley, and Jean Brodie as examples of acting expertise. Her ability to blend comedy with tremendous emotional depth has made her a case study of what it takes to genuinely embrace a character.

Retrospectives of Maggie's work will almost surely continue to emerge on stages and screens for years to come, with theater groups and film festivals devoting whole seasons to her extensive repertoire. The British Film Institute has already organized a retrospective event, celebrating her contribution to both stage and cinema, solidifying her position in British cultural history. Meanwhile, her work in television notably in Downton Abbey continues to draw in new viewers, indicating that her appeal spans generations and time.

Beyond her talent, Dame Maggie Smith's humanitarian endeavors and discreet support for philanthropic organizations will also constitute a big part of her legacy. She was recognized for sponsoring institutions that encouraged the arts, but her efforts stretched well beyond the public eye. Through contributions and lobbying, she worked behind the scenes to aid children's organizations, arts foundations, and cancer research, causes that were near to her heart. Her compassion, like her skill, will live on, impacting people in ways that stretch beyond her roles.

In her last interviews, Maggie constantly stressed that she never desired celebrity for fame's sake. It was always about the labor, the craft, and the relationship with her characters. And now, as fans, critics, and colleagues reflect on the immense influence of her life, it's apparent that her humility, commitment, and amazing skill will continue to inspire for many decades to come. Through her indelible performances, her profound personal elegance, and her modest generosity, Maggie Smith's soul will remain a valued part of cultural history and an icon for all years.

In conclusion, the world may have bid farewell to Dame Maggie Smith, but her presence will never completely leave us. Her life's work continues to amaze, educate, and inspire. Just as the theater and cinema will never forget her, neither will the millions of admirers whose lives were touched by the brilliance, knowledge, and love she gave to every character she portrayed.

APPENDIX

Filmography:

A complete and detailed list of Dame Maggie Smith's extensive work across film, television, and theater. Her career spanned over seven decades, with notable highlights across all mediums.

Films:

- *Nowhere to Go* (1958) – Her film debut
- *The Prime of Miss Jean Brodie* (1969) – Academy Award for Best Actress
- *Murder by Death* (1976)
- *A Room with a View* (1985) – BAFTA Award for Best Actress in a Supporting Role
- *The Lonely Passion of Judith Hearne* (1987)

- *Sister Act* (1992) and *Sister Act 2: Back in the Habit* (1993)
- *The Secret Garden* (1993)
- *Harry Potter* series (2001-2011) – as Professor Minerva McGonagall
- *The Best Exotic Marigold Hotel* (2011) and its sequel (2015)
- *Downton Abbey* (2019) – Film adaptation of the series

Television:

- *Downton Abbey* (2010-2015) – as Violet Crawley, the Dowager Countess of Grantham
- *Talking Heads* (2020) – A revival of Alan Bennett's series

Stage Productions:

- *The Importance of Being Earnest* (1960) – Old Vic Theatre
- *Private Lives* (1972) – National Theatre

- *Lettice and Lovage* (1987) – Role for which she won a Tony Award
- *The Lady in the Van* (1999) – later adapted for film
- *A German Life* (2019) – Her final stage role

Awards and Accolades:

Dame Maggie Smith's extraordinary career has been recognized with numerous awards and honors. Below is a full list of her major nominations and wins.

Academy Awards:

- 2 Wins:
    - *The Prime of Miss Jean Brodie* (1969) – Best Actress
    - *California Suite* (1978) – Best Supporting Actress
- 6 Nominations

BAFTA Awards:

- 5 Wins:
    - *The Prime of Miss Jean Brodie* (1969)
    - *A Private Function* (1984)
    - *A Room with a View* (1985)
    - *The Lonely Passion of Judith Hearne* (1987)
    - Special Award (1993)

Golden Globe Awards:

- 3 Wins:
    - *California Suite* (1978)
    - *A Private Function* (1984)
    - *Downton Abbey* (2012)

Tony Awards:

- 1 Win:
    - *Lettice and Lovage* (1990) – Best Actress in a Play

Screen Actors Guild Awards:

- 3 Wins for *Downton Abbey* (2012, 2014, 2016)

Honorary Awards:

- Dame Commander of the Order of the British Empire (1990)
- Companion of Honour (2014)

Quotes by Maggie Smith:

Dame Maggie Smith was not only known for her incredible acting but also for her wit and insightful perspectives, both in her interviews and her roles. Here are some memorable quotes from her:

From her roles:

- *The Dowager Countess* (Downton Abbey):
    - "What is a weekend?"
    - "Don't be defeatist, dear, it's very middle class."

From her interviews:

- On acting: "I longed to be bright and most certainly never was. I was rather hopeless, I think."
- On aging: "It seems to me there's this terrible pressure to put on this front of eternal youth and I think it's so pathetic."
- On her career: "I am deeply grateful for the work. But I was never driven by fame. I always wanted to work, and I was just lucky enough to be in the right place at the right time."

This appendix serves as a testament to Dame Maggie Smith's monumental contributions to entertainment, both on-screen and off. Through her unforgettable performances, distinguished awards, and deeply thoughtful words, her legacy continues to resonate with audiences worldwide.

Request for Reviews

Thank you for taking the time to explore this in-depth journey through the life and legacy of Dame Maggie Smith. As a reader, your opinion holds immense value, and your feedback can help shape the experience for future readers. ***I kindly request that you leave a review sharing your thoughts on the book.*** Whether it's reflecting on the life of this iconic actress or commenting on the style and depth of the narrative, your insights are crucial.

Reviews not only provide valuable feedback for me as the author, but they also help new readers discover the book and appreciate the profound influence Dame Maggie Smith had on the world of cinema and theater. Whether you ***loved certain chapters, found new perspectives, or felt moved by her story,*** I encourage you to share your experience.

Thank you again for being part of this journey. ***Your review is greatly appreciated and will help keep Dame Maggie Smith's*** legacy alive through the stories we tell.

Thank you for your time and thoughts!

Printed in Great Britain
by Amazon